**Traditions and Superstitions**

# HOCKEY'S Best TRADITIONS and WEIRDEST SUPERSTITIONS

by Elliott Smith

CAPSTONE PRESS
a capstone imprint

Published by Capstone Press, an imprint of Capstone
1710 Roe Crest Drive, North Mankato, Minnesota 56003
capstonepub.com

Copyright © 2023 by Capstone. All rights reserved. No part of this publication may be reproduced in whole or in part, or stored in a retrieval system, or transmitted in any form or by any means, electronic, mechanical, photocopying, recording, or otherwise, without written permission of the publisher.

SPORTS ILLUSTRATED KIDS is a trademark of ABG-SI LLC. Used with permission.

Library of Congress Cataloging-in-Publication Data
Names: Smith, Elliott, 1976- author.
Title: Hockey's best traditions and weirdest superstitions / by Elliott Smith.
Description: North Mankato, Minnesota : Capstone Press, an imprint of Capstone, [2023] | Series: Sports Illustrated Kids: Traditions and Superstitions | Includes bibliographical references and index. | Audience: Ages 8-11 years | Audience: Grades 4-6 | Summary: "Going to a hockey game? Don't leave before the handshake line. And if you're in Detroit, be sure to buy an octopus before the game. But first, hit the ice to discover the ins and outs of good sportsmanship, good fun, and good luck in hockey. With engaging text and striking photos, this book will delight young sports fan with some of the best and weirdest practices on the ice and in the stands"-- Provided by publisher.
Identifiers: LCCN 2022008483 (print) | LCCN 2022008484 (ebook) |
ISBN 9781666346633 (hardcover) | ISBN 9781666346640 (pdf) |
ISBN 9781666346664 (kindle edition)
Subjects: LCSH: Hockey--Miscellanea--Juvenile literature.
Classification: LCC GV847.25 .S545 2023 (print) | LCC GV847.25 (ebook) | DDC 796.356--dc23/eng/20220427
LC record available at https://lccn.loc.gov/2022008483
LC ebook record available at https://lccn.loc.gov/2022008484

Editorial Credits
Editor: Ericka Smith; Designer: Tracy Davies; Media Researcher: Svetlana Zhurkin; Production Specialist: Katy LaVigne

Image Credits
Associated Press: Cal Sport Media/John Crouch, 17, Cal Sport Media/Richard Ulreich, 22, Elise Amendola, 19, Fred Jewell, 10, Gene J. Puskar, 21, Marcio Jose Sanchez, 15 (top), Scott Audette, 11, ZUMA Wire/Cal Sport Media/David McIntyre, 27; Getty Images: Bruce Bennett, 7, Rich Lam, 12; Newscom: Cal Sport Media/Kostas Lymperopoulos, 13, Icon SMI APA/Christopher Szagola, 8, Icon SMI/Steven King, 16, ZUMA Press/Douglas R. Clifford, 23, ZUMA Press/Tampa Bay Times/Dirk Shadd, 29, ZUMA Press/Valery Sharifulin, 25; Shutterstock: 3DMI, cover (top left), Bonma Suriya, 4, Dan Kosmayer (puck), cover and throughout, DGIM studio (burst background), cover and throughout, Dzha33, cover (red and blue baseball caps), Jai Agnish, 20, Klara Steffkova, 28, Leonard Zhukovsky, 9, Mega Pixel (rat), cover (middle right), Mott Jordan, cover (title fonts), Pixfiction, cover (green baseball cap), QiuJu Song, cover (bottom right), Sergey Panychev, 5 (bottom), Shelbyagility (rats), cover (bottom), 15, Yellow Cat, cover (top right); Sports Illustrated: Damian Strohmeyer, 5 (top), Erick W. Rasco, 26

All internet sites appearing in back matter were available and accurate when this book was sent to press.

Direct Quotation
Page 19, from Sept. 8, 2016, NESN article, "Cam Neely, Bruins 'Very Excited' About New 'Overdue' Practice Facility," nesn.com

Printed in the United States     5398

# TABLE OF CONTENTS

**INTRODUCTION**
**FROZEN FUN** . . . . . . . . . . . . . . . . . . . . . . . . . 4

**CHAPTER 1**
**IN-GAME TRADITIONS** . . . . . . . . . . . . . . . . . 6

**CHAPTER 2**
**STADIUM FUN** . . . . . . . . . . . . . . . . . . . . . . . 14

**CHAPTER 3**
**SUPERSTITIONS** . . . . . . . . . . . . . . . . . . . . . 18

**CHAPTER 4**
**PLAYOFF AND OLYMPIC PRESSURE** . . . . . . 24

**GLOSSARY** . . . . . . . . . . . . . . . . . . . . . . . . . . 30
**READ MORE** . . . . . . . . . . . . . . . . . . . . . . . . 31
**INTERNET SITES** . . . . . . . . . . . . . . . . . . . . . 31
**INDEX** . . . . . . . . . . . . . . . . . . . . . . . . . . . . . 32
**ABOUT THE AUTHOR** . . . . . . . . . . . . . . . . . 32

Words in **bold** are in the glossary.

## INTRODUCTION

# FROZEN FUN

Hockey is played all over the world. Players and fans follow many of the same rules and traditions no matter where the puck drops. From Canada to Malaysia, unbelievable **feats** on the ice make the game an amazing experience. And a bit of fun off the ice adds to the excitement.

## WINTER CLASSICS

Many National Hockey League (NHL) stars say playing outdoor hockey as kids helped fuel their love for the game. Skating outside is still special for many league players. That's why the NHL started its Winter Classic series in 2008. Each year, the league hosts a game at an outdoor stadium. It's one of the most popular days of the season.

# CHAPTER 1

# IN-GAME TRADITIONS

The action on the ice is fast and furious. Nifty skaters, crunching hits, and speedy slap shots can keep fans entertained. But beyond the rapid-fire line changes and clever one-timers, there are lots of traditions that add to the fun. So don't blink. You might miss some important traditions!

## ROOKIE RITUAL

For hockey players, nothing is more exciting than their **debut**. But in the NHL, a rookie's teammates often have a few tricks up their sleeves.

Teams will let a rookie lead the pregame skate before their first game. But they won't actually follow him. They'll stay behind for a little while. This leaves the rookie skating a few laps alone in front of the crowd. It's the team's way of welcoming the player to the league.

But the tradition can be embarrassing. During his rookie lap in 2021, Minnesota Wild forward Brandon Duhaime stepped on a stray puck and fell!

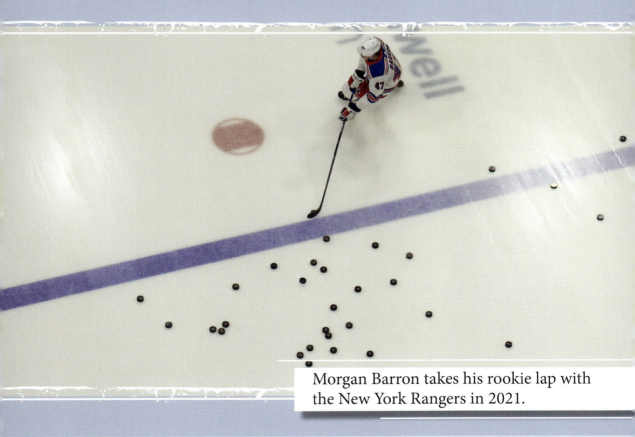

Morgan Barron takes his rookie lap with the New York Rangers in 2021.

### WHO'S THE GOALIE?

Want to know which goalie will play first? Watch the teams come out for warm-ups. The starting goalie will be the first person on the ice.

# TAP, TAP, TAP

Hockey players wear a lot of equipment. Thick gloves are important pieces of gear. But wearing them makes clapping for a good play or a goal hard. So players have to get creative.

Players use their sticks to celebrate. They tap their sticks on the ice or the boards in front of their bench. Players also tap their sticks to honor former players and during pregame ceremonies.

## RAISE 'EM HIGH

After a big win, players will raise their sticks in the air. This is how they recognize the fans' support.

The U.S. Women's Hockey Team celebrates a win during the 2018 Winter Olympics.

# THE HORN BLOWS

When a team scores a goal, the celebration begins. At most NHL arenas, this means a horn will blow loudly. It seems normal now, but the horn celebration wasn't always a part of the game.

In 1973, the Chicago Blackhawks became the first NHL team to use a goal horn. Their owner liked the sound of the horn on his **yacht**. He decided to install one at the stadium. Fans loved it!

The Chicago Blackhawks in 1973

Other teams didn't take up this tradition right away. Eleven years passed before another team began sounding a goal horn. Now, all 32 NHL teams use a horn to celebrate goals. Since the horns are different shapes and sizes, they make different sounds.

# THREE STARS

After the final buzzer, hockey teams honor the players who had the biggest impact on the game. Three players are called back from the locker room for one final skate. They are announced as the three stars of the game. Sometimes players from the opposing or losing team are recognized too.

This practice dates back to 1936. It started as an advertisement for an oil company that sponsored the NHL. After the sponsorship ended, the practice continued. Now, members of the local media select the stars.

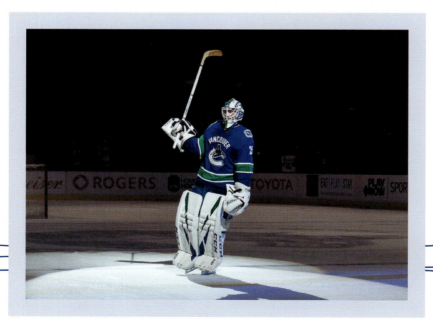

Jacob Markström of the Vancouver Canucks is named a star after a 2019 win against the Calgary Flames.

Joel Ward is recognized as the first star of a 2014 Washington Capitals game.

## CHAPTER 2
# STADIUM FUN

Fans play a big role in making a hockey game fun. Die-hard fans follow many traditions. Whether they're finding creative ways to celebrate a goal or show their support for a team, fan traditions add to the thrill of attending a game.

## HATS OFF

Scoring three goals in one game is extremely difficult. It's so remarkable that the feat has earned a special name—a hat trick. The term actually comes from the game of **cricket**.

In hockey, when a player scores three goals, fans throw hats onto the ice. The arena staff collect the hats. Then the game continues.

At a 2018 Anaheim Ducks game, fans threw hats onto the ice after Ondrej Kase scored three goals.

What happens to the hats? Teams have different plans. Some put the hats on display. Others donate them to charity. A few offer the hats to the player. And some let fans reclaim their hats.

### RAT TRICK

Panthers fans took the hat trick to a new level in the 1990s. A Panthers player revealed he killed a rat with his stick in the locker room. He then scored two goals during the game that day. Fans were inspired. They started bringing plastic rats to throw onto the ice whenever the Panthers scored.

# OCTO-TOSS

One of the most unique traditions in hockey began in 1952. A Detroit Red Wings fan **smuggled** something special into a game. He threw it onto the ice to represent the eight wins Detroit would need to claim the Stanley Cup. It was an octopus!

After the Red Wings won the championship, a tradition was born. Fans began throwing octopi onto the ice during the playoffs. The tradition soon expanded to the regular season, even when the Red Wings were on the road!

When Detroit closed its old arena in 2017, octopi were tossed onto the ice. It was a fitting farewell.

## COLOR RUSH

Fans will do almost anything to inspire their teams. Many teams have organized color nights to create a memorable visual experience. During the Winnipeg Whiteout, fans wear all white. This tradition, which started in 1987, creates a blizzard-like effect. Washington Capitals fans wear red as their rallying color. Their support helped the Capitals win the Stanley Cup in 2018.

# CHAPTER 3
# SUPERSTITIONS

Hockey players are very superstitious. They might not admit it, but many have routines they follow every game.

## DON'T STEP HERE!

The locker room is a special place for a hockey team. It's where the players gather to prepare for the game. And nearly all locker rooms have a team **logo** in the center of the floor.

Teams consider it bad luck to step on the logo when entering the locker room. Some teams have the logo taped off.

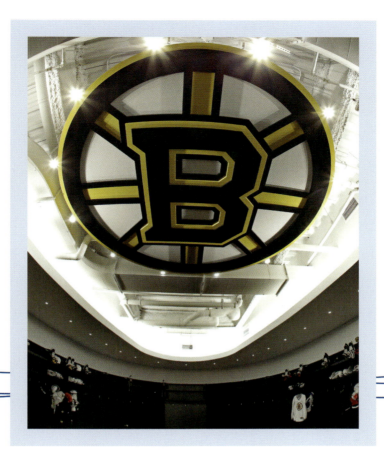

The Boston Bruins have moved their logo to the ceiling for maximum safety. "I don't know why the logo is on the floor," Bruins president Cam Neely said. "The whole concern about people stepping on it seemed to take up a lot of energy. I just felt it was time to move it."

### TAP THE GOALIE

Nearly all players take part in tapping the goalie before each game. During the pregame skate, players will swing next to the goalie and touch the goalie's pads with their sticks for good luck.

# CROSBY'S STICKS

Sidney Crosby is one of the NHL's best players. The Pittsburgh Penguins center is also one of its most superstitious players. Crosby has many routines. He's one of the last players out of the tunnel. He practices shooting from the same spot on the ice. And when the team travels, he sits in the same seat on the team's plane.

Most importantly, Crosby will not let anyone touch his sticks after he has taped them. If someone does, he will retape them to get the good vibes back.

Crosby tapes his stick during a 2021 game.

# AVOID THE TROPHY

For NHL players, winning the conference finals is thrilling. That means they're going to the Stanley Cup Finals. After a conference win, the team gets a trophy. But most players will ignore it.

Some players consider touching the conference trophies bad luck. They believe it will jinx them and they won't win in the finals. Some teams will skate around the trophy but not touch it. But others have tempted **fate** and grabbed the trophy to celebrate. The Tampa Bay Lightning touched their conference trophies in 2020 and 2021. And they still won the Stanley Cup both years!

Tampa Bay Lightning players touch the Eastern Conference trophy in 2021.

## CHAPTER 4

# PLAYOFF AND OLYMPIC PRESSURE

When games are really important, hockey players respond in unique ways. Some start new rituals just for the playoffs. Others rely on familiar routines.

## CHICKEN PARMESAN, PLEASE!

Alex Ovechkin of the Washington Capitals eats the same meal during home playoff games. He orders chicken parmesan, pasta, bread, and four separate sauces—alfredo, meat, mushroom marsala, and marinara.

# OLYMPIC DREAMS

Hockey players love to participate in the Olympics. They show their national pride and compete for bragging rights. And they bring their traditions and superstitions with them.

For some members of the U.S. Women's Hockey Team, superstitions are huge. In 2018, they were willing to do whatever it took to beat their rival Canada and win gold.

Goalie Maddie Rooney got a little help from a handful of longstanding practices. One of them is wearing a headband she's had since she was 12 years old. Another is putting her left pad, left sock, and left skate on first. Her rituals worked. Rooney helped the United States beat Canada 3–2.

Rooney (left) and teammate Nicole Hensley celebrate their win during the 2018 Olympics.

# PLAYOFF BEARDS

Why do NHL players look so scruffy during the playoffs? It's because of a tradition that has been growing since the 1980s.

In 1980, the New York Islanders started growing beards at the start of the playoffs. By the end of the decade, the team had won four Stanley Cups. Other teams noticed. Before long, playoff beards were common.

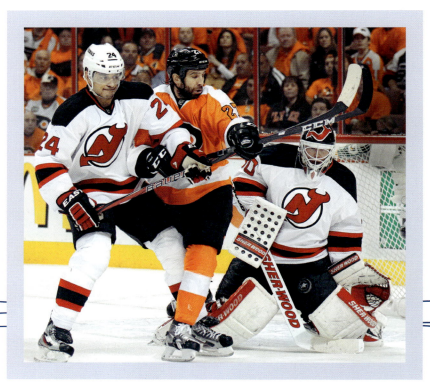

Maxime Talbot (middle) of the Philadelphia Flyers wears a playoff beard during a game against the New Jersey Devils in 2012.

## HANDSHAKE LINE

Hockey is known as a rough sport. But the players still practice good sportsmanship. The best example of that is the handshake line.

After NHL playoff series and other competitions, players don't head to their locker rooms right away. Instead, the players will shake hands at center ice. It's a way to acknowledge a well-played series.

No one knows when this tradition started. But it has become an important part of the game.

# A DAY WITH THE CUP

The team that wins the Stanley Cup each year knows it's the best team in hockey. The players also get to have the coolest trophy in sports.

Every player and staff member of the team that wins the Stanley Cup can have the trophy for one day. They can do whatever they want with it. Some have taken it to their hometowns. Others have eaten food out of it. And a few have brought it on fishing trips. In 2021, the Lightning dented the Stanley Cup during a riverboat party. But after some repairs, it was back in action!

The Lightning's Alex Killorn (seated) and Nikita Kucherov show off the Stanley Cup in 2021.

## MARKED IN HISTORY

The names of every player who has won the Stanley Cup are etched into the trophy. New rings are added to the cup to fit additional players as the years pass, and older rings are removed and sent to the Hockey Hall of Fame. The trophy is 35.25 inches (89.5 centimeters) tall and weighs 34.5 pounds (15.6 kilograms).

# GLOSSARY

**cricket** (KRI-kuht)—an outdoor bat-and-ball game that is similar to baseball

**debut** (DAY-byoo)—a person's first appearance

**fate** (FAYT)—events in a person's life that are out of that person's control

**feat** (FEET)—an achievement that requires great courage, skill, or strength

**logo** (LOH-goh)—a visual symbol for a company or a team

**smuggle** (SMUHG-uhl)—move something secretly and often illegally

**yacht** (YOT)—a large boat or small ship used for sailing or racing

# READ MORE

Gish, Ashley. *Ice Hockey*. Mankato, MN: Creative Education, 2022.

Hewson, Anthony K. *GOATs of Hockey*. Minneapolis: Abdo Publishing, 2022.

Storden, Thom. *Hockey's Greatest Nicknames: The Great One, Super Mario, Sid the Kid, and More!* North Mankato, MN: Capstone, 2022.

# INTERNET SITES

*National Hockey League*
nhl.com

*Sportsnet: Hockey 101*
sportsnet.ca/hockey/hockey-101/

*USA Hockey*
usahockey.com

# INDEX

Barron, Morgan, 7
Boston Bruins, 19
Chicago Blackhawks, 10
Crosby, Sidney, 20–21
Detroit Red Wings, 16
Eastern Conference, 23
Hensley, Nicole, 25
Hockey Hall of Fame, 29
Kase, Ondrej, 15
Killorn, Alex, 29
Kucherov, Nikita, 29
Markström, Jacob, 12
Neely, Cam, 19
New York Islanders, 26
Olympics, 9, 25
Ovechkin, Alex, 24
Rooney, Maddie, 25
Stanley Cup, 16, 17, 22, 26, 28–29
Talbot, Maxime, 26
Tampa Bay Lightning, 22, 23, 28, 29
U.S. Women's Hockey Team, 9, 25
Ward, Joel, 13
Winnipeg Whiteout, 17
Winter Classic, 5

# ABOUT THE AUTHOR

Elliott Smith is a freelance writer, editor, and author. He has covered a wide variety of subjects, including sports, entertainment, and travel, for newspapers, magazines, and websites. He has written a nonfiction book about the Washington Nationals and a children's book about Bryce Harper. He lives in the Washington, DC, area with his wife and two children.